Outlearning the Wolves

Surviving and Thriving in a Learning Organization

by David Hutchens

illustrated by Bobby Gombert

PEGASUS COMMUNICATIONS, INC.

Waltham

PEGASUS
COMMUNICATIONS

Outlearning the Wolves: Surviving and Thriving in a Learning Organization
by David Hutchens; illustrated by Bobby Gombert
Copyright © 1998 by David Hutchens
Illustrations © 1998 Pegasus Communications, Inc.

Library of Congress Cataloging-in-Publication Data
Hutchens, David.
Outlearning the wolves: surviving and thriving in a learning organization /
by David Hutchens; illustrated by Bobby Gombert.
p.   cm.
ISBN 1-883823-24-2
1. Organizational learning—Problems, exercises, etc.   I. Title.
HD58.82.H88   1998
658.4'06—DC21   97-53299
CIP

Acquiring editor: Kellie Wardman O'Reilly
Project editor: Lauren Johnson
Production: Boynton Hue Studio

Printed on recycled paper.
Printed in the United States of America.
First printing, March 1998.

Outlearning the Wolves
Volume Discount Schedule
1–4 copies $19.95 each • 50–149 copies $13.97 each
5–19 copies $17.96 each • 150–299 copies $11.97 each
20–49 copies $15.96 each • 300+ copies $9.98 each

Prices and discounts are subject to change without notice.

Pegasus Communications, Inc.
One Moody Street
Waltham, MA 02453-5339
Phone: (781) 398-9700
Fax: (781) 894-7175
www.pegasuscom.com

5196

02 01 00 99   10 9 8 7 6 5 4

For Robbie

The First Chapter

This is a wolf.

This is a sheep.

Wolves eat sheep.

Any questions?

Wolves have always eaten sheep.
They always will eat sheep.
If you are a sheep, you accept this as a fact of life.

———•———

A flock of sheep once lived together in a beautiful, green pasture.

But the flock's existence was not a peaceful one. The wolves posed a constant threat, casting a shadow of fear over the pasture.

Sometimes, the flock would settle in to sleep at night and awake in the morning to find one of them was gone—likely being served up to a wolf with asparagus tips and mint jelly.

There were several miles of sharp, barbed-wire fence that surrounded the sheep's fields.

But the wolves came anyway.

It was hard to live amid such uncertainty.

Still, over the years, the flock got bigger and bigger and bigger. The occasional loss, though very sad, was to be expected.

This was the way
it had always been.

Another Chapter

This is Otto.

You should know that Otto will face an untimely demise by the end of this story.

Don't get too attached to him.

Otto was saddened by the rest of the flock's resignation to the wolves.

"I have a dream . . . " said Otto, perched on a hill where the rest of the flock could hear him. "I dream of a day when not another sheep will ever die to become breakfast for a wolf."

"That is absurd," said Shep the sheep. "You cannot stop the wolf. Remember the inspiring words of our ancestors: *'The wolf will come, just as the sun will rise.'* And also: *'Wolves. What jerks.'"*

"Indeed, I believe we are to be *commended*," said another sheep. "For we have prospered beneath the shadow of the wolf. Just look at how many of us there are!"

This made Otto even sadder.

"As long as the wolf is present, our strong numbers tell us only a half-truth," said Otto. "We tell ourselves we are strong so we won't have to face up to the ways we are weak."

Otto continued: "We all say the wolf cannot be stopped. But how do we *know* this is true?"

A sheep named Curly answered, "It *is* true. Why, even the fence that surrounds us cannot keep the wolves away. At first, it stopped them. But they must have learned to jump over it. Wolves learn very quickly," Curly added.

"Then *we* must learn—even more quickly!" said Otto. "We must make learning an ongoing part of life in the flock. We will become a *learning* flock."

"But we *do* learn," said Shep, mildly indignant. "Why, just the other day, I learned to pull a thorn out of my hoof with my teeth." (All the other sheep—especially those with thorns in their hooves—raised their woolly eyebrows in interest.)

"And I have learned to dig a hole. Watch this!" said Gigi, as she began vigorously clawing at the ground.

"Uh ... I can push rocks around with my nose to make a pile," offered Jerome, who was just barely following the conversation.

An excited murmur arose among the sheep at these new insights, which, though perhaps obvious to you and me, were quite innovative and useful in the sheep world.

"This learning is a good start," said Otto, a little encouraged. "Ideas like these must be shared for the benefit of the flock."

"But to thrive in the shadow of the wolf, it is not enough. We need a different kind of learning if we are to be a true learning flock."

The flock looked down, sheepishly. They were trying hard to understand.

After some silence, Curly spoke. "Perhaps we could sleep in a circle."

Otto motioned for her to continue.

"Well," said Curly, "I think we could protect ourselves better if we slept in a huddle and not scattered all over the place. That way, when the wolves come, it will be harder for them to get us."

"But that doesn't really address the problem of the wolves . . . " said Marietta, a little lamb. But no one heard her. The sheep were too excited by Curly's idea.

"Yes, yes!" they all said. "Tonight we will huddle against the wolves. *Learning* may be a good idea after all!"

Otto was frustrated by the sheep's attempt at learning, which, to him, seemed awfully reactionary. But he felt relieved to see them at least united in purpose. This was a good first step. "The least I can do," he thought, "is stay awake tonight and keep guard while they sleep."

[WARNING! This brings us to the part of the story where Otto cashes in his chips. Take comfort in knowing that he is going to a better place where he will join Lassie, Old Yeller, and Bambi's mother.]

That night, Otto watched as the sky darkened and the sheep gathered together into a huddle. By the time the crescent moon was high in the summer sky, the flock had fallen fast asleep.

The next morning, Otto was gone.

Yet Another Chapter

When the flock woke the next morning to find Otto gone, they were devastated.

"Otto was a good sheep," sighed Shep.

"He showed us a vision of a better day," eulogized Curly.

"He had fleece as white as snow," someone said from the back.

Jerome didn't say anything. He just pushed a bunch of rocks into a pile with his nose—perhaps not the most effective coping mechanism, but it seemed to work for him.

But the mood soon turned sour.

"Those wolves! This is all their fault!" moaned Curly.

"What are we supposed to do?" cried Shep. "The wolves are smart, and they are strong, and they cannot be stopped. Our lives would be so much better if there were no wolves."

"If only that stupid fence were taller, so the wolves could not jump over it."

The flock sat there, dejected and miserable.

Finally, Marietta, the little lamb, spoke again.

"How come the wolves only come sometimes, and not all the time?" she asked the flock.

Everyone stopped. They looked confused.

Marietta continued. "If wolves are smart, and they can jump over the fence anytime they want, how come they don't come *every* night? If I were a wolf, that's what *I* would do. I would feast on sheep all the time."

The others looked even more confused.

"All I'm saying," said Marietta, "is that maybe the wolves aren't as unstoppable as we think. *Something* is stopping them, at least some of the time."

"What are you getting at, Marietta?" asked Shep.

"I'm saying the same thing Otto said. We must learn. We must do it together. And we must learn faster than the wolves."

"We tried being a learning flock already," said Shep. "And look where it got Otto."

"That's because we've only just started," said the wise little lamb. "Look at what just happened: We tried something *different,* but the results we got were the same. What does that tell you?"

Everyone had to admit that it was a pretty good question. But no one had an answer.

Marietta explained: "It tells *me* it isn't enough just to change the way we do things. We must also broaden our vision, and see the bigger picture. We need to learn *how to learn differently.*"

"How?" everyone wanted to know.

"We can start by doing three things:

"One, remember Otto's vision. *Someday, not another sheep will ever die because of wolves.* From now on, everything we learn must lead us toward Otto's vision.

"Two, everyone says that wolves are too smart, and cannot be stopped. We have made all of our decisions thinking that this is true, and maybe it is. *But what if it isn't?*

"Three, let's figure out how to do things differently. What do we have to do to stop the wolves? What is it like to *be* a wolf? Let's go out and get some ideas and information. Let's find out as much about the wolves as we can. Then, let's share everything we know with each other.

"Why don't we each do some thinking on our own, and then meet here this afternoon to talk?"

The meeting adjourned, and the sheep all went their separate ways, lost in thought.

Some of the sheep struggled with what Marietta had said:

"Learning may be all well and good. But if that fence isn't tall enough to keep out wolves, there is nothing we can do. We don't have the tools to make it taller."

"I won't stand for this kind of disrespect to our ancestors. They taught us that wolves were a fact of life. That little ewe is making a mockery of our heritage."

But some of the sheep took what Marietta said to heart:

"Marietta is right. The wolves only seem to come at certain times. That doesn't make sense."

"Last summer, when we had the drought, the wolves seemed to come much more often. Hmmmm...."

"Maybe the wolves *aren't* jumping over the fence. It's pretty high ... and I don't think any animal is *that* strong...."

Later that afternoon, all the sheep came back together to talk. A feeling of excitement buzzed among them. (Impressed by the turnout, Jerome made an attempt to count the sheep ... but, strangely, he found himself becoming so sleepy that he had to stop.)

Shep began the meeting. "Friends, we are here today in memory of our friend Otto, and his vision to eliminate one hundred percent of deaths due to wolf attacks. Does anybody have anything to share?"

The sheep shared all their thoughts.

They engaged in a dialogue on whether a wolf could really jump over the fence.

They discussed the strange timing of WRCs (Wolf-Related Casualties), and how they seemed to decrease after hard rains and increase during hot and dry periods.

They even confessed how difficult it was for them to rethink their own long-held beliefs about wolves.

Just talking about these things energized the flock and gave them hope.

Suddenly, Curly came trotting up, out of breath but very excited.

"Follow me! Hurry!" she said.

Confused, the sheep ran off after her, not at all sure where Curly was leading them.

The Final Chapter

The flock hurried after Curly for about a mile. Soon they came to the fence, right at the spot where a small stream ran underneath it. This was the same stream where the sheep often drank—although never this close to the fence, for fear of wolves.

"Look!" Curly said, pointing with her hoof to the spot where the fence crossed over the water. There, just above the surface of the water and caught on the barbed wire, was a small clump of sheep's wool.

"I was looking around for answers and I found this—but I don't know what it means," she said.

The sheep looked at each other in confusion.

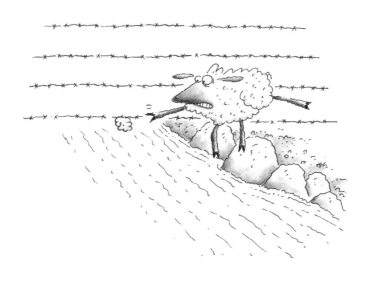

Finally, someone spoke up. "I got it! The wolves aren't going over the fence. They're going *under* it!"

Another sheep excitedly added, "*That* makes sense! When there is a drought, there is no water going under the fence. That's when the wolves crawl under!"

"And after it rains, there's too *much* water, and the wolves can't go under," exclaimed another.

The sheep got even more excited.

"So I guess that means . . . *wolves can't swim!*" Everyone laughed heartily at this.

Perhaps the wolves weren't so smart after all.

"There's only one problem," someone said. "We can't control when it rains. We're still at the mercy of the wolves. And now we're at the mercy of the weather, too."

The flock fell quiet.

Then Gigi spoke. "I think we're looking at the wrong problem again.

"It's true that we can't control the weather. But we *can* control the flow of the water. Watch this." And Gigi began to dig a hole, vigorously pawing at the ground under the fence with her hooves. Soon, some of the other sheep joined in.

"Don't just stand there! Everybody help!" someone called.

"Well . . . I can push rocks around with my nose to make a pile," Jerome offered, and began building a small dam with rocks, a few feet downstream.

Shep stood by, pulling thorns out of the hooves of other sheep as they dug.

Soon, a small pond began to form around the fence.

Amazed by this achievement, the sheep let out
a spontaneous, collective bleating sound (an
extremely irritating noise, but it sounds
joyful if you're another sheep).

In the days that followed, the flock had a beautiful
pond around which they could gather and drink
and play.

But best of all, the wolves stopped coming . . .

. . . the sheep stopped disappearing . . .

. . . and the fear was gone.

"I'm glad we became a learning flock," the sheep would later say, as they nestled safely in to sleep at night.

"It feels good to know that we'll never have to go through anything like that ever again."

But maybe they would.

The End

A Closer Look at *Outlearning the Wolves*

Right now, you may be asking yourself: "Why did I just spend my valuable time reading a fairy tale about sheep and wolves and learning?"

Good question. Don't let the fun tone of *Outlearning the Wolves* fool you. A big part of learning is having fun—and metaphors like the one you just read are valuable ways to illuminate new truths about the world in which we live.

And the sheep in the story have some important ideas to share— ideas that can have a far-reaching impact on the way organizations do business on a global scale, as well as the way you do your work on a day-to-day basis.

Toward a Learning Culture

What is a learning culture? How does one go about institutionalizing this culture? And what is meant by "learning"?

In the story, Shep the Sheep was a little defensive when Otto introduced the idea of learning. "But we do learn," Shep protested. Defensiveness is a natural reaction. To say we must become a learning culture might seem to imply that up until now, *we have not been learning.* But that's not necessarily true. Instead, the challenge facing organizations is to make learning *institutional,* by defining and building organizational capabilities and structures for learning, such as culture, processes, systems, and skills.

Remember at the beginning of the story when the sheep displayed skills such as digging holes and removing thorns from their hooves? Those were valuable skills, but with no culture, processes, or systems in place, the skills existed in a vacuum. The skills had never been brought together and leveraged for the greater good of the flock. You can see how the sheep may have all learned individually—but it wasn't until learning was aligned, made deliberate, and *institutionalized* that they surpassed even their own expectations. They were then able to build a pond that raised their quality of existence and expanded their capacity to grow.

The challenge that faces learning organizations is to institutionalize learning so that groups can create the future they want, together. And for many organizations, the surface has barely been scratched. Just as the sheep discovered, there are always opportunities for further growth. Taking (or even *seeing*) those opportunities requires learning.

Making Learning Happen

Whether you are a flock of sheep or a global company, there are three areas in which organizational changes must take place in order for a learning culture to emerge.[1]

◆ **Guiding Ideas** is one area. Every organization is governed by ideas, vision, values, and purpose—whether these are openly  stated or not. A guiding idea may be *climb the corporate ladder* or *make as much money as you can.* (Hopefully, the guiding ideas are more inspiring.) In the story, the sheep were initially governed by a passive, unspoken guiding idea: We are victims, and merely to survive is success. Otto introduced a new and empowering guiding idea: "I dream of a day when not another sheep will ever die to become breakfast for a wolf."

That new vision catalyzed some strikingly different behaviors within the flock.

Note, though, that this guiding idea is not an ideal one, because it is self-terminating. In other words, once the wolves have been shut out, then what? A more compelling guiding

1. Model is from Peter Senge, in *The Fifth Discipline Fieldbook* (Doubleday, 1994), pp. 15–47.

idea might lift the aspirations of the flock beyond the message of simply "not dying." (Also, note the potential problems that could come from tinkering with real-life predator/prey systems. Increasing the number of sheep or decreasing the number of wolves could create imbalance in the environment, resulting in chaos. Systems thinking—a concept that we will be touching on in just a few minutes—can shed some light on these complex dynamics.) Despite their less-than-ideal vision, give Otto and the flock some credit. They are just beginning their learning journey.

A *learning culture* brings with it many new and challenging guiding ideas—like *"I cannot operate independently from an organization,"* and *"The way I perceive the world actually affects the reality of the world."* It truly is a new way of approaching the world, and its implications strike at a deeply personal and individual level. Perhaps you can see why learning is an unsettling experience for many.

◆ **Theory, Methods, & Tools** is another area that must be addressed to foster a culture of learning. These represent a *new way of thinking*.

Guiding Ideas

Theory, Methods, & Tools

Domain of Action

Marietta broke significant ground when she introduced a radical new theory: *What if it isn't true that wolves are unstoppable?* It was a courageous act—just as it is when anyone challenges deeply held convictions. (Remember the sheep who said, "She's making a mockery of our heritage"?)

Introducing new theory is just the beginning. Methods and tools are also important for testing and working within the new theory. Again, the efforts of the flock in the story are relatively simple ones; during the flock's final meeting, for example, the sheep admit their difficulty in challenging their own beliefs and share some of the information they have learned. This dialogue was a new method of communication for the sheep.

◆ **Innovations in Infrastructure** is the final realm of change for a learning culture. How will people in organizations access all of the new ideas, theories, methods, and tools? How can they work together to benefit from the learning culture? Indeed, how will people go about fostering the learning culture to begin with? These questions point to the need for *infrastructure.*

Guiding Ideas

Innovations in Infra-structure

Theory, Methods, & Tools

Domain of Action

One example of infrastructure can be seen in Marietta's speech to the flock on page 33. She said, "Let's find out as much about the wolves as we can. Then let's share what we learn with one another." In other words, the sheep's new infrastructure involved an information-gathering and -sharing network. That's about as basic as you can get—but it is an infrastructure nonetheless. In the sheep's case, this simple innovation produced some dramatic shared learning.

How can companies help foster the learning infrastructure? One common mistake is to treat *learning* as a program. Learning is not something that can be "rolled out" with seminars, training manuals, banners, and coffee mugs. (In fact, the abandonment of the "training seminar" approach may be, for many, another innovation in infrastructure.) Instead, learning is a business-driven effort that we may choose to adopt at an individual level. If a learning culture takes hold in an organization, it will be because of people like you who are committed to learning and growing.

Growing the Culture, One Sheep at a Time

Learning is a *discipline.* On one level, it means a new way of *doing* things. But more important, it's a new way of *being* and *seeing.* (This is one reason why the "training seminar" approach often fails to build a learning culture. Learning takes place in a realm of *experience,* not from a flip chart.) For people who engage in this kind of learning, a profound experience occurs that might be described as an "awakening." Such people literally see the world and their place in it differently.

The flock of sheep dug a pond that kept out the wolves and raised their quality of existence. It was an extraordinary team achievement—but if you look closer, you'll see that the behaviors and results stemmed from an *individual* level. The flock changed because the individual sheep changed. That change took place in three areas:

◆ **New Skills and Capabilities.** How do people know whether they are learning? Easy. According to Peter Senge, author of *The Fifth Discipline* and co-author of *The Fifth Discipline Fieldbook* (two seminal texts on the principles of the learning culture), we know we are learning "when we can do things we couldn't do before." For example, the fact that Jerome learned to push rocks around with his nose was, in fact, legitimate learning. (At least, for him it was.) Transferring that skill into the new context of building a dam to create a pond to protect the flock from wolves was an even higher level of skill building and learning for Jerome.

Skills &
Capabilities

Domain of Change

◆ **New Awareness and Sensibilities.** New skills and capabilities lead to new awareness and sensibilities. Think of these as enhanced insights, or deeper understandings of systems—insights that cause you to question assumptions and observations that may appear obvious.

For example, some of the sheep realized that "the wolves don't come after the rain, and they come more often when it is hot and dry." Wasn't this obvious? Why didn't the sheep realize this sooner? Surely there were many opportunities over the years to observe this pattern.

Maybe not. The reason the sheep missed this "obvious" pattern is that *it did not match their picture of reality*. It was only at Marietta's insistent urging to challenge the belief ("We all say the wolves cannot be stopped ... *but what if it isn't true?*") that the sheep were able to "see" and then explore this

Skills &
Capabilities

Awareness &
Sensibilities

Domain of Change

readily available information. (More specifically, the sheep who were able to suspend their biases were able to see the information.)

◆ **New Attitudes and Beliefs.** New awarenesses ultimately lead to new beliefs. At the end of the story, the sheep had a collective realization: *Maybe the wolves aren't so smart after all. Maybe they* really *can be stopped.* Is it surprising that this new belief radically changed things for the flock? Think about it: The person who lives life believing he could die at any moment has a very different experience of life than the person who believes she is relatively safe from harm. The flock's beliefs about the world had a very powerful effect on the way they experienced the world. When the way you view the world around you

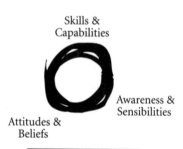

Skills &
Capabilities

Awareness &
Sensibilities

Attitudes &
Beliefs

Domain of Change

changes, *the world itself changes, too.* The flock's new belief about their world had immediate, tangible results. Their lifestyle ("confidence replaced their fearful existence ... "); their future ("wolves stopped coming ... sheep stopped disappearing ..."); and even the landscape of their pasture all changed. The story is a metaphor for the real power that is available to organizations in which individuals are constantly growing and learning.

So Where Do I Begin?

In his book *The Fifth Discipline: The Art & Practice of the Learning Organization,* Peter Senge details at considerable length five disciplines that individuals and organizations must adopt to create a true learning culture.

Briefly, the five disciplines are:

◆ **Systems Thinking.** Events in our lives are rarely as simple and direct as they appear. Systems thinking is the practical application of *system dynamics*—an intricate field of study that examines the patterns and structures that govern nature, families, the economy, our bodies, companies, and all other systems. The flock's original cause-and-effect view of the world might be "wolf gets hungry, wolf eats sheep." But the sheep discovered that a more complex system was in play, where variables such as the weather, the wolves' limitations, and the flock's own biases all interacted and influenced one another in complex cause-and-effect relationships. Broader knowledge of this larger system gave the sheep the power to change it.

◆ **Personal Mastery.** Personal mastery is the ability to create the results you want with an economy of means. People with a deep sense of personal mastery are on an ongoing journey of self-discovery. Through our limited observance of Otto and Marietta, we see hints of this trait. After all, they were both willing to challenge conventional thinking, confront the flock, and involve themselves in the learning. People without commitment to personal mastery are doomed to be victims of the world around them. (Remember the sheep's complaint, "If only the stupid fence were taller . . . !")

◆ **Mental Models.** A mental model is a deeply held vision or set of beliefs and assumptions about the world. You have mental models; it is impossible *not* to have them. These are all examples of mental models:

—*People are basically trustworthy.*

—*Our organization has maxed out its potential.*

—*I'll be happy when I am married/promoted/etc.*

—*The wolves cannot be stopped.*

The truth or falsity of the above statements is beside the point. Mental models are not inherently good or bad—they are simply our brains' way of sorting through an endless stream of information and putting it in a context so as to make sense of the world.

The fact is, once you adopt a worldview, you may have a very difficult time opening it to challenge—especially if you are unaware of the existence of your mental model. Interestingly, simply *believing* any of the statements listed above may actually make them true *for that person.* That's the principle of "the self-fulfilling prophecy."

Mental models hold a great deal of power over us. However, in a learning culture, individuals can release the fierce need to defend and justify their mental models and become adept at challenging and "trying on" new ones. Exploring yours and others' is a great way to gain new insights and build a broader understanding of the complex world around you.

◆ **Shared Vision.** Senge says, "When there is genuine vision (as opposed to the all-too-familiar 'vision statement') people excel and learn, not because they are told to, but because they want to." Building true shared vision has been the challenge of leadership over the ages. In the case of the sheep, we see both resistance to and acceptance of the vision. Indeed, if Otto's vision had not literally been a matter of life and death, the flock's resistance might have been even greater.

◆ **Team Learning.** When a team far exceeds what could have been accomplished individually, no matter how brilliant the individual team members may be, that team is experiencing team learning. Also, when teams are truly learning, the individual members are growing more rapidly than they could have otherwise. The phenomenon of an organization accomplishing something extraordinary (like sheep creating a pond) requires a *dialogue* in which team members can share ideas and challenge each other, and individuals can set aside their own defensiveness.

This is just a glimpse at the disciplines that must come together in order for a learning organization to emerge. And now we're back to the original question: *So where do I begin?*

Here are a few ideas:

◆ Examine your own mental models. What is *your* equivalent to "the wolves can't be stopped"?

◆ Share your learning. Reflect upon how the metaphor in *Outlearning the Wolves* might apply directly to your own organization. Share your thoughts with others who are interested in the principles of the learning culture.

◆ Learn more. Are you intrigued by the promises of the learning culture? Find out more about it. Peter Senge's *The Fifth Discipline* is a good place to start.

Remember, learning is a journey. It is not a skill or a technique; it is a discipline. It's a way of looking at the world. It is about growth and discovery.

The sheep came together to create a peaceful and prosperous existence, centered around a serene pond in a meadow.

What reality would you like to create?

Other Titles by Pegasus Communications

Learning Fables
Shadows of the Neanderthal: Illuminating the Beliefs That Limit Our Organizations

The Pegasus Anthology Series
Making It Happen: Stories from Inside the New Workplace

Managing the Rapids: Stories from the Forefront of the Learning Organization

The New Workplace: Transforming the Character and Culture of Our Organizations

Organizational Learning at Work: Embracing the Challenges of the New Workplace

Reflections on Creating Learning Organizations

The Pegasus Workbook Series
Systems Archetype Basics: From Story to Structure

Systems Thinking Basics: From Concepts to Causal Loops

The "Billibonk" Stories
Billibonk & the Thorn Patch

Frankl's "Thorn Patch" Fieldbook

Billibonk & the Big Itch

Frankl's "Big Itch" Fieldbook

Human Dynamics
Human Dynamics: A New Framework for Understanding People and Realizing the Potential in Our Organizations

Newsletters
THE SYSTEMS THINKER™

LEVERAGE®: News and Ideas for the Organizational Learner

The Innovations in Management Series

Pegasus Communications, Inc. is dedicated to providing resources that help people explore, understand, articulate, and address the challenges they face in managing the complexities of a changing world. Since 1989, Pegasus has worked to build a community of organizational learning practitioners through newsletters, books, audio and video tapes, and its annual *Systems Thinking in Action®* Conference and other events. For more information, contact:

Pegasus Communications, Inc.
One Moody Street
Waltham, MA 02453-5339
Phone: (781) 398-9700   Fax: (781) 894-7175
www.pegasuscom.com